WESTCHESTER PUBLIC LIBRARY
P9-EMH-511

Lisa
of
Willesden
Lane

Lisa
of
Willesden
Lane

A True Story of Music and
Survival During World War II

MONA GOLABEK and LEE COHEN

Abridged and adapted by
Sarah J. Robbins

Illustrations by
Olga and Aleksey Ivanov

Ⓛ Ⓑ

LITTLE, BROWN AND COMPANY
New York Boston

Lisa of Willesden Lane was adapted for young readers by Sarah J. Robbins. It is an abridgment of *The Children of Willesden Lane: Young Readers Edition* by Mona Golabek and Lee Cohen and adapted by Emil Sher, published by Little, Brown Books for Young Readers.

Copyright © 2021 by Mona Golabek
Illustrations copyright © 2021 by Olga and Aleksey Ivanov
Discussion Guide copyright © 2021 by Mona Golabek and
Hachette Book Group
Photographs courtesy of Mona Golabek

Cover art copyright © 2021 by Olga and Aleksey Ivanov. Cover design by Jenny Kimura. Cover copyright © 2021 by Hachette Book Group, Inc.

Hachette Book Group supports the right to free expression and the value of copyright. The purpose of copyright is to encourage writers and artists to produce the creative works that enrich our culture.

The scanning, uploading, and distribution of this book without permission is a theft of the author's intellectual property. If you would like permission to use material from the book (other than for review purposes), please contact permissions@hbgusa.com. Thank you for your support of the author's rights.

Little, Brown and Company
Hachette Book Group
1290 Avenue of the Americas, New York, NY 10104
Visit us at LBYR.com

First Edition: January 2021

Little, Brown and Company is a division of Hachette Book Group, Inc. The Little, Brown name and logo are trademarks of Hachette Book Group, Inc.

The publisher is not responsible for websites (or their content) that are not owned by the publisher.

Library of Congress Cataloging-in-Publication Data
Names: Golabek, Mona, author. | Cohen, Lee, author. | Robbins, Sarah J., other. | Ivanov, O. (Olga) illustrator. | Ivanov, A. (Aleksey) illustrator.
Title: Lisa of Willesden Lane: a true story of music and survival during World War II / Mona Golabek and Lee Cohen; abridged and adapted by Sarah J. Robbins; illustrations by Olga Ivanov and Aleksey Ivanov.
Description: New York: Little, Brown and Company, 2021. | Audience: Ages 6-10 | Summary: "The true story of a girl who traveled on the Kindertransport during World War II and her experiences during a time of war"—Provided by publisher.
Identifiers: LCCN 2020041430 | ISBN 9780316463072 (hardcover) | ISBN 9780316463065 (paperback) | ISBN 9780316540407 (ebook) | ISBN 9780316500869 (ebook other)
Subjects: LCSH: Golabek, Lisa Jura—Childhood and youth—Juvenile literature. | Pianists—England—Biography—Juvenile literature. | Jews, Austrian—England—Biography—Juvenile literature. | Jewish refugees—England—Biography—Juvenile literature. | LCGFT: Biographies.
Classification: LCC ML3930.G63 G67 2021 | DDC 786.2092 [B]—dc23
LC record available at https://lccn.loc.gov/2020041430

ISBNs: 978-0-316-46307-2 (hardcover), 978-0-316-46306-5 (pbk.), 978-0-316-54040-7 (ebook)

Printed in the United States of America

LSC-C

Hardcover: 10 9 8 7 6 5 4 3 2 1
Paperback: 10 9 8 7 6 5 4 3 2 1

Printing 1, 2020

♫

This book is dedicated to
young readers everywhere.

May Lisa's story inspire you
to find the music within
your heart and the dream
you wish to follow.

Contents

A Note from the Author

My mother, Lisa, was my best friend and my teacher. She taught my sister, Renée, and me to play the piano. She would always say to me, "Mona, each piece of music tells a story." And in those piano lessons, she told me the story of her life.

Lisa was a young refugee from Austria who boarded the Kindertransport and left her home and her family just before World

War II. She never forgot what her mother (my grandmother) told her on a cold December day in 1938 at the Vienna train station: "Lisa, hold on to your music, and I will be with you every step of the way."

My mother found a new home and new friends in a Jewish hostel on Willesden Lane in the northern part of London. As the war broke out, she fueled Britain's war efforts with long hours at the sewing machine in the East End factories. As bombs from the Blitz rained down on London at night, she pounded out the chords of the Grieg piano concerto, determined to keep her promise. That music gave her the strength to face an uncertain future, while inspiring all the other Jewish refugee children who lived in the hostel with her.

I decided to write this book to help readers think through important questions: *What do you hold on to in life when facing great challenges? What is our purpose? How do we help our fellow humankind?*

I have shared this story with thousands of students across the globe, and in turn, young people have shared the impact of the story on them. "We connect with Lisa and the violence she faced," a high school student from Chicago wrote. But the student added, "If Lisa can do it, I can do it." During a school visit in California, a student told me, "I don't know yet what I want to do with my life, but this book has helped me decide what kind of person I want to be."

Like my mother, the heroine of this book, I hope that others will discover the courage to be a hero in their own lives.

Kindertransport Routes

Lisa
of
Willesden
Lane

Chapter One

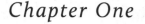

Lisa Jura boarded the streetcar and headed across the city for her piano lesson with Professor Isseles.

She loved the ride.

Every Sunday since her tenth birthday, the fourteen-year-old girl left her home in the Jewish section of Vienna, Austria, and made the trip. It felt like going back in time, to a city of grand palaces and great composers like Mozart and Beethoven. Lisa dreamed of living up to their legacy.

As the streetcar passed Symphony Hall, Lisa closed her eyes and imagined sitting at the piano in the great auditorium. She straightened her back as her mother had taught her, took a breath, and pretended to play.

Lisa's daydream ended when she heard the driver calling out her stop. His words were strange and different: "Meistersinger Street." Why hadn't he said, "Mahler Street," as usual?

Lisa climbed down into the great plaza to see that all the street signs had changed. The Nazis, the prejudiced political party that now held power in Austria, did not want such a grand avenue named after Gustav Mahler, a Jewish composer.

At the professor's old stone building, Lisa was surprised to see a German soldier blocking the doorway.

"What business do you have here?" he asked coldly.

"I have a piano lesson," she replied, trying not to be frightened.

From the second-floor window, the professor waved to say that it was all right for the girl to come up. Frowning, the soldier allowed Lisa to pass.

♪♩

Lisa was relieved to see Professor Isseles. For the next hour, she could forget everything and be a part of the music she loved.

Placing the score of Beethoven's *Moonlight Sonata* on the music stand, she sat on the worn piano bench and began to play. The white-haired professor followed along with his copy of the music.

For most of the hour Lisa played, the old man sat in silence. She'd hoped he would smile. After all, he'd said she was his best student. Why did he look so upset? Was she playing that badly?

"I am sorry, Miss Jura. But there is a new law," he said slowly when she had finished. "It is now a crime to teach a Jewish child."

Stunned, Lisa felt tears rising.

"I am not a brave man," he said softly. "I can no longer teach you. I am so sorry."

He picked up a thin gold chain that held a tiny charm in the shape of a piano.

"Never forget your remarkable gift, Lisa,"

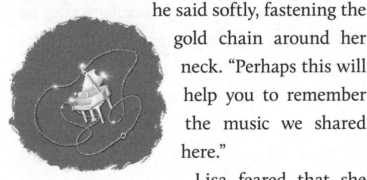 he said softly, fastening the gold chain around her neck. "Perhaps this will help you to remember the music we shared here."

Lisa feared that she would never see her teacher again. She thanked him, collected her things, and then turned and ran.

Lisa shivered in the cold November wind. Why were the Nazi Germans telling Austrians what they could or couldn't do? It wasn't fair, and why were the Austrians letting them?

She couldn't wait to get back to Franzensbrücken Street in her Jewish neighborhood. There, everyone knew her as the little girl who played the piano. The neighbors who could hear her music in the butcher's shop or the bakery called her by that special word: a prodigy.

Music was Lisa's whole world: an escape from the run-down flats, shops, and markets. And now, it was the most important escape of all: from the Nazis.

When Lisa got home, her mother, Malka, sensed that something was wrong. She held her daughter, who was crying. Malka guessed

WHAT IS NAZISM?

The National Socialist German Workers' Party, or Nazi Party, gained power in Germany after World War I. Their leader, Adolf Hitler, was a powerful dictator who hated Jewish people—a dangerous belief known as anti-Semitism. In March 1938, Nazi Germany took over Austria, including Lisa's hometown of Vienna. The Nazi Party passed laws that excluded Jews economically, culturally, and socially.

what must have happened. "Is it Professor Isseles?" she asked.

Lisa nodded.

"Don't worry, I taught you piano before. I will teach you again," Malka said, even though both of them knew that Lisa could now play more complicated music than her mother could.

"Come," Malka said. She pulled out some music by the composer Chopin and sat at the piano. "I'll play the right hand, you play the left," she said.

Lisa played the four-four rhythm of the marching, repeating chords. After she'd mastered the left hand, she took over from her mother, who watched proudly.

When they finished, Lisa went to her room and cried into her pillow. She soon felt a warm hand on her shoulder: her twenty-year-old sister, Rosie. "Don't cry, Lisa," she urged. "Let me show you something I just learned." She led Lisa into the bathroom, where makeup was spread out on the bathroom dresser. "I'll show you a new way to do your lips."

Their twelve-year-old sister, Sonia, burst through the door. "Look at Lisa," Rosie said. "Doesn't she look like a movie star?"

Lisa stared excitedly at her new face in the mirror. She looked five years older!

Soon they heard footsteps. Rose hid the makeup, while Lisa scrubbed her face with soap and water. Little Sonia looked on and giggled. For a moment, the sorrow of parting from Professor Isseles seemed far away, and the three sisters joined hands and emerged to greet their mother.

♫

Later, Lisa went to the window of their second-story apartment, peering into the cobblestone courtyard.

"Do you see him?" Malka yelled from the kitchen.

"No, Mama, not yet."

Lisa's father, Abraham Jura, was a proud man who had always called himself "the best tailor in all Vienna." But now that the Nazi Party forbade non-Jews from using Jewish tailors, he had fewer customers. Sometimes, after she had gone to bed, Lisa heard her parents arguing about money. She noticed that the stress was slowly pushing Papa away. Gone were the early-evening dinners and the bear hugs when Papa came home from work.

It was Friday, at sunset. Shabbat, the Jewish day of rest, was beginning, with or without her father. Malka lit two white candles in silver holders, then four more—one for each of her three daughters and one for her own mother, Briendla, in Poland. A warm yellow light filled the room.

Lisa's mother had a tradition of feeding poor neighbors on the night of the Sabbath. People usually lined up in the hallway an hour before sunset. But this evening, Malka went into the hallway and said sadly, "I am afraid we have nothing to share tonight."

After dinner, Malka sat under the window in a large mahogany rocking chair. She rocked slowly back and forth, reciting her prayers, eyes focused on the street below.

♫

A few nights later, Lisa and Sonia awoke to the sound of distant shouting.

They ran to the living room window and saw the sky red with the flames of burning buildings. Above the shouting came the piercing sound of shattering glass. Nazi soldiers in brown shirts were running down the block.

Lisa pulled Sonia back into the bedroom they shared. "Get under the bed and stay there!" Rosie had gone to the home of her fiancé, Leo, so Lisa ran into the hallway to search for her mother.

"Lisa!" She heard the cry on the stairwell and ran down to find her mother holding her father's head in her lap. He was bleeding.

"It's only a small cut, Lisa, don't worry," her father said when he saw her terrified expression.

Malka cleaned Abraham's cuts with a warm towel. Lisa gently picked shards of glass out of the folds of his clothing as he told them what had happened.

"On my way home, I saw people smashing

windows and writing nasty words in paint. I ran past the synagogue. They were taking the scrolls and the Torah out into the street and setting them on fire!"

Lisa couldn't believe his terrifying words.

There were no sirens, he told them: "They wanted everything to burn." It was the night that came to be known as Kristallnacht—the Night of Broken Glass. Nazis would kill one hundred Jewish people, set fire to nearly two hundred synagogues, and destroy thousands of Jewish homes and businesses throughout Germany, Austria, and Czechoslovakia.

From their window, the family could see that the house on the corner was on fire. Abraham laced up his shoes and ran down the stairs to help.

They watched and watched until Malka could no longer bear it. She led her two girls to the bedroom, where they waited in silence for the terrible night to end.

Chapter Two

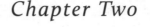

Jewish people were no longer allowed on the streets at night. They couldn't go to movie theaters, concert halls, or most other public places.

As Adolf Hitler, the leader of the Nazi Party, became more powerful, he encouraged Nazi soldiers to continue their attacks on stores and homes. Abraham's tailor shop on the first floor was now closed by government order. Although twelve-year-old Sonia still went to school, she was no longer allowed to talk to any of her friends who weren't Jewish. The day her best friend stopped speaking to her, Sonia came home crying.

One night, Lisa crept out of bed and stood in the hallway, listening to her parents talk. She heard the words *Holland* and *England*.

"We must do something immediately. The chance may not come again." her father said.

Everyone in Vienna had been talking about the Kindertransport—the Children's Train. While the Nazis had forbidden Jews from leaving Vienna, they did allow some trains to take Jewish children under the age of seventeen away to safety in England. The British people—Jews and Christians alike— volunteered to help the children in homes and hostels. Every Jewish family in Vienna wanted seats on those trains to save their children. Now Papa had managed to get one ticket!

"Hundreds of children have already gone," he said. "My cousins Dora and Sid live in London. This could be our only chance."

Lisa could hear her mother gasp. "So, you

WHAT WAS THE KINDERTRANSPORT?

The Kindertransport was a series of actions by British organizations and others to rescue Jewish children from Greater Germany following Kristallnacht, the Night of Broken Glass. Ten thousand children were allowed by the British government to enter Great Britain, and on December 2, 1938, the first train with two hundred children arrived. Of the ten thousand children rescued, over seven thousand were Jewish. Many of the children became citizens of Great Britain or emigrated to other countries. Most of them would never see their parents again.

are asking me to send my precious daughters away?"

"Malka, there is only one place, for only one child, right now," said Abraham unhappily. "We must send Lisa or Sonia. Rosie is over their age limit. As soon as we are able, we will find a way to send the others."

Malka walked out of the kitchen and smiled sadly at her daughter. "Go to bed now, my darling."

Lisa kissed her mother's cheek and walked back to her bedroom. She saw Sonia sleeping peacefully next to her rag dolls and wondered what the decision would be.

♫

The next morning, Lisa was reading at the kitchen table when her parents entered the room.

"We have made a decision," her mother said. "You are strong, Liseleh, and you have your music to guide you. We will send you first. As soon as we can find enough money, we will send your sisters."

Then Malka began to cry.

Lisa was silent. She felt like crying, too, but she wanted to be strong.

"There is a place called the Bloomsbury House that has arranged for Jewish children to come to England. It's safer there," said her father.

"Can't we wait and go together?" Lisa asked.

Abraham looked tenderly at his daughter. "Sonia will come next, and then Rosie and Leo and your mother and I will join you. Your cousins will take care of you until we get there."

Hanukkah, the Festival of Lights, came in the middle of December. Since Jews were no longer allowed on the streets without a special pass, the family lit the menorah and said their prayers alone each night. The Kinder-transport was scheduled to leave a week later.

The morning of her train's departure, Lisa awoke before anyone else. She walked through the house, determined to remember everything she loved. She brushed her fingers in the air above the piano's keys. Then she rolled up her sheet music of "Clair de Lune" and put it in her suitcase.

The Westbahnhof train station was crowded with hundreds of desperate families pushing toward the waiting train. Nazi soldiers in long brown coats stood by the door of each train car. They shouted into bullhorns as they inspected suitcases and papers.

Abraham stopped to hand Lisa her small suitcase. It was time to say goodbye. But Lisa could only clutch the handle and stand frozen.

He put his arm around Rosie, easing her toward Lisa. The two sisters hugged.

"Take the window seat so we can see you," Rosie shouted above the noise. "We'll all be together again soon. Be brave for us."

Next, Lisa kissed Sonia. She reached into her pocket and slipped Professor Isseles's tiny gold charm around Sonia's neck.

"Keep this for me until I see you again."

Abraham hugged Lisa so tightly she could hardly breathe. He was crying, something she had never seen him do before.

Malka guided her through the crowd toward the platform. Some of the children lined up were Lisa's age, some older, some younger, carrying toys and dolls. Teary-eyed parents buttoned their children's coats, brushed their hair, and laced up untied shoes.

When it was Lisa's turn to board the train, Malka held her close.

"You must hold on to your music," her mother said. "Please promise me that."

Lisa sobbed, "How can I do that without you?"

She dropped her little suitcase and hugged her mother tightly.

"You can and you will. Remember what I've taught you. Your music will help you through—let it be your best friend, Liseleh. And remember that I love you."

At the guard's command, Lisa headed for the steep metal stairs. She felt Malka slip a little envelope into her hand. Before she knew it, she was carried along onto the train car.

Lisa quickly got to a window seat and waved. The train began to move, and then everything disappeared into steam and smoke.

In the envelope was a photograph of Malka, standing straight and proud on the day of Lisa's last recital at school. On the back was written, *From the mother who will never forget you.*

As the train gathered speed, Vienna shrank

into the distance. The city that she knew and the family that she loved were gone.

♫

Lisa hoped she'd see someone from her school, from her neighborhood, from her synagogue. Yet the train was filled with strangers.

Each child wore a tag with a number around the neck. Lisa's number was 158. The train stopped several times in the night, and more and more children got on. Lisa felt determined. *If I can keep strong*, she thought, *I can make it. I'll make it for Mama and I'll make it for Papa. And soon we will all be together again.*

After many hours, a long, shrill whistle sounded, and the train stopped again. Someone saw a sign out the window.

"It's in Dutch! The sign is in Dutch! We must be at the border!" It was a bright, moonlit night. Through the window Lisa saw the windmills turning slowly—like those in the picture books Papa had shown her.

They had arrived at the Hook of Holland, a town on the North Sea. Women climbed aboard carrying baskets filled with fat slices of fresh-baked bread and butter and big, doughy shortcake biscuits. One lady balanced a tray of steaming mugs of cocoa. Forgetting their manners, the children devoured the treats.

Soon they were led through the small station and across the large, busy road to the seaport. There, a bearded old seaman smiled and waved them along the dock toward the ramp. "Hurry along and up. Next stop is England."

Lisa turned for a moment and looked down at the Dutch town, with its rows of thatched roofs. It didn't look the least bit like Vienna. *Where will we end up?* she wondered as she boarded the ship.

For what seemed like hours, Lisa lay awake on the top bunk, looking out of the tiny porthole. The moon had disappeared. It was impossible to tell where the water ended and the sky began.

When she finally slept, she dreamed of home. In her dream, Mama was serving brisket and Papa was at the head of the table, ready to carve. Sonia was there, noisy and impatient, and so was Rosie, stately and beautiful. One chair was empty. "Where is Lisa?" her father asked. From deep inside her sleep, Lisa tried to respond.

"Here I am," she cried, but no one heard her as the waves of green water drowned out her voice.

♫

By morning, they reached the other side of the English Channel. The single-file line of more than two hundred children walked down the gangplank. They gripped their little suitcases so tightly, it was as if they carried their hearts inside.

A wiry man with a dark blue coat and a walrus mustache hurried them along. "There's a train to catch! Let's look lively. Hurry along."

As they wound through the center of the tiny English village, Lisa looked back at the sea that separated her from her family and all she had ever known.

Chapter Three

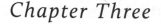

The train rumbled through the English countryside. Fields gave way to suburbs, and then to stone buildings. Finally, they reached their destination—Liverpool Street station in London, England.

The exhausted children were met at the station by a group of nuns, rabbis, and Red Cross workers carrying clipboards. "Welcome to England! We're delighted to have you," the

Red Cross workers sang as they checked their lists. Lisa sighed with relief: Her name was on the list that had been prepared by Blooms-bury House, a Jewish refugee rescue organization active during World War ll.

After waiting for what seemed like hours, Lisa saw a small man in a worn brown over-coat, holding a photo. He came up and spoke to her in Yiddish.

"Lisa Jura?" He introduced himself as her father's cousin, Sid Danziger.

But instead of hugging her, he bowed his head and said quietly, "My wife just had a baby, so we're leaving the city. We won't be able to take you. We're very sorry."

Lisa didn't know what to say. These were her relatives, her cousins, the only people that she knew in all of England.

"What about Sonia?" she asked, panicked. She had hoped they might sponsor her little sister as well.

"We'll ask our friends. We're not wealthy people. I'm sorry."

Though disappointed, Lisa knew that Mama would have wanted her to be polite. "Thank you for coming to tell me," she managed.

"It's the least I could do," he said sadly, before turning to walk away.

♫

Lisa was put on a bus to the Bloomsbury House. When she got off, she saw Englishmen in pinstripe suits and shiny bowler hats walk by, looking just like the pictures she had seen in her schoolbooks.

Inside, children were everywhere. Phones were ringing and people were shouting in languages she didn't understand. Women passed around cucumber sandwiches—something Lisa had never seen.

Children were called in, one at a time, for

interviews prior to being placed with a family. When it was Lisa's turn, she met a tall and balding man behind the desk. He peered over his glasses and motioned for her to take a seat.

"I'm Alfred Hardesty. Nice to meet you."

Lisa smiled politely.

"How are you feeling?"

"Very well," she said in her best English pronunciation.

"Glad to hear it. Bloomsbury House tries to help children like you during this difficult

time. We can also find you a job so you can earn extra money. Does that interest you?"

"Oh, yes, yes."

"Good. Now, what sorts of things can you do?"

"I play the piano," Lisa said proudly.

"I'm sure you play beautifully, but what do you do that would be more useful? Do you sew?"

"Yes, I do."

"Good," Mr. Hardesty said, and checked a little box on the form he was filling out.

"I have a sister...in Vienna."

Mr. Hardesty looked at the long line of children before him.

"All in good time, Miss Jura," he said with a sigh, and stood to gently walk her out.

♫

Older girls were placed first, since they could work and pay their way. Small children were chosen next by childless couples. The rest waited to be sent to hostels and orphanages that were being readied by Quakers, Jewish groups, churches, and kind souls from all over England. On the third day, Lisa was called to the office.

"Miss Jura?" began a stout English lady. "We understand you like to sew, which is excellent. Do you get along with young children?"

The woman explained that an important military officer was opening up his home to aid the war effort. "They need some extra help," she said. "What do you think, dear?"

Lisa quickly agreed. She was thrilled—she'd make the rich family love her right away, and then they'd help her and eventually Sonia, too.

"It's all settled, then, young lady. Someone will meet you at the station when you arrive in Brighton tomorrow."

That night, she pulled out the photo of her mother. Then she unfolded a sheet of paper and began to write to her family. Lisa filled the letter with positive thoughts and English phrases she hoped would impress them. For the first time since her arrival in England nearly a month before, she had hope.

♫

The next morning at the Brighton by the Sea train station, a chauffeur named Monty picked her up in an elegant black car and drove her to a huge country estate. It looked like a castle out of her daydreams—three stories tall, with turrets crowning the left and right corners.

A cook, three maids, and a butler came out to meet her. "Welcome to Peacock Manor," said a lady with a no-nonsense air about her. "I'm Gladys. Come in and take a hot bath, and we'll get you some tea."

Gladys showed Lisa to a small room in the servants' wing and gave her a starched white maid's uniform. Later she took her to the study to meet her sponsor, Captain Richmond.

"So there you are, missy. Good to have you here. You make sure Gladys treats you nicely!" The captain, a man in his sixties, winked good-naturedly at the head maid.

"Thank you," said Lisa.

Gladys handed Lisa a feather duster. "Just follow along and keep your eyes open," she said.

♪♫

Not long after, Lisa was introduced to Captain Richmond's wife, the lady of the house. Soon, Lisa was given a job as the lady's maid. Lisa vowed to be useful and cheerful at all times. At sunrise she was in her crisp uniform, hard at work. She scrubbed floors, fetched coal, and dusted endlessly. Her only purpose: to make the money her parents needed to send Sonia to England.

But behind Lisa's cheerful smile was deep concern about her family: In the three months since she had been in England, she had heard nothing to ease her worries. Hitler had already taken over Austria, and the news from the rest of Europe was upsetting.

A few days later, Monty handed her a letter marked 13 Franzensbrücken Street, in her mother's handwriting. Lisa was overjoyed. *Make us proud of you; we miss you every day*, Lisa's mother wrote. Monty put his arm around her when the tears came.

One night, she heard loud voices coming from the captain's study next door.

"I told you this is what it would come to!" a man's voice shouted.

Then Lisa heard the voice of Hitler on the radio, echoing through the manor house.

The captain walked into the hall, waving his arms in disgust, and spotted Lisa. "Aha!" he said. "Come here, we need you to translate."

He took her arm gently and led her into the room, where five men in uniforms sat in front of the radio.

"What is this maniac saying now?" he asked.

Lisa heard Hitler's hateful words through

the radio. An officer, seeing her distress, exclaimed, "Have a heart, don't make the poor girl listen to this."

"All right, dear, that's enough. Thank you," the captain said.

But Lisa had already seen evil deeds during Kristallnacht. Those images she could not erase from her mind.

HOW DID WORLD WAR II BEGIN?

The German army continued taking over European countries in 1939. When the German army invaded Poland, Britain and France declared war. Many other countries, including the United States, eventually joined the fight. Together, they became known as the Allied powers. The German side, which included Italy, Japan, and others, was known as the Axis powers. This long war, which ended with the German and Japanese surrender in 1945, is known as World War II because it was the second war to involve many countries across the globe.

One morning, after Lisa laid out the outfit she had chosen for the lady of the house, she took a deep breath. "Madam? May I ask you something?"

"Certainly. What is it?"

"I have a sister in Vienna. She's twelve. She's very sweet and she could work in the kitchen. Could you sponsor her, too?"

The lady frowned.

"She'd be no trouble, I promise. She's very well behaved...."

The lady gave her a sad smile. "Unfortunately, we cannot. I'm sorry."

♫

Lisa tossed and turned that night as she came up with a plan. The next morning, she joined Gladys and Monty on their trip into the village for supplies. On her way out, she stuffed her pocket with the envelope that held her wages.

When they arrived, Lisa walked into the secondhand shop where she had seen a bicycle in the window. She told the shopkeeper that she wanted to buy it.

"You must be the refugee I've been hearing about! Four pounds, two shillings," he said, picking up the tag. "Hmm, seems a bit pricey for what it is. How does two pounds sound?" he asked with a wink.

Lisa pulled money from her envelope and handed it to the man. "Can you keep it here until I come to get it?" she asked.

"Whenever you need it, it'll be here."

Chapter Four

After her next payday, Lisa rose before dawn and packed her things. With a pencil she found in the kitchen, she wrote carefully, *Thank you. I will never forget you, but I must go.*

She collected her red bike at the second-hand shop and tied her small suitcase to the back. The sun was just breaking through the morning fog as she took off from the village. A sign read BRIGHTON—45 KILOMETERS.

Lisa was excited—she was returning to Bloomsbury House, where they could find a place for her in the big city and she could find a way to bring Sonia there. But as she pedaled, her doubts grew. Should she have left a house with caring people who fed and sheltered her? Would she even make it to London?

At nightfall she arrived at Brighton's station, only to find out that the next train wouldn't leave until the following day.

Wheeling her bicycle through the station, she hung her head. Finally, she found a small wooden bench in the ladies' room. She lay down on it and put her head on her suitcase. She was too tired to dream.

♫

The next morning, Lisa awoke to the sound of a flushing toilet. She grabbed her things and ran onto the platform, to the waiting train. She took one last glance back at her red bicycle before boarding.

After arriving at Waterloo station, Lisa followed the careful directions of helpful pedestrians and walked the many miles to Bloomsbury House.

"We were worried," said Mr. Hardesty when he saw her. "The captain told us you'd gone missing. Were they treating you badly?"

Lisa's face reddened. "No, sir."

"Were you getting enough to eat?"

"Yes, sir."

Mr. Hardesty sighed.

Lisa began the speech she had rehearsed in her head. "Excuse me, sir, I came back to London because I don't want to be a maid. I play the piano and I am going to make something of my life. Please," she begged, "let me stay in London."

Mr. Hardesty's face softened. "Let me see what I can do, at least temporarily." He picked up the phone. "Mrs. Cohen? Alfred Hardesty here, Bloomsbury House. I know I promised not to send so much as one more sardine your way, but there's a lovely young lady who just needs a place for a month...."

Lisa could hear the raised voice of a woman from her seat. Cupping his hand over the mouthpiece, Mr. Hardesty leaned forward and said, "I think you two will get along just fine."

♫

Mr. Hardesty escorted Lisa to her new home: the hostel at 243 Willesden Lane, where an imposing middle-aged woman in a dark purple dress opened the door.

"Please come in!" she said. "Let's not stand here while the house fills up with flies."

With Lisa's suitcase in his hand, Mr. Hardesty gently guided her through the doorway.

The house's dark-paneled foyer opened into a pleasant drawing room. Stepping farther inside, Lisa saw a distinctive shape, covered with a hand-crocheted shawl.

Her heart beat faster. A piano!

"We're overcrowded, you know. We can only make room for you temporarily," Mrs. Cohen said, not noticing Lisa's expression of wonder. "I'll have one of the girls tell you the rules."

Gina, a pretty, dark-haired girl with bright eyes, bounded down the stairs. "You must be the new girl."

"Yes, I'm Lisa Jura."

"Pleased to meet you!" she said with an exaggerated bow. "Isn't my English fabulous? That's the first rule: Mrs. Cohen says you have to speak English on the first floor at all times. There are millions of rules, but don't worry, I'll go over everything."

Gina started running back up the stairs. "Come on! I'll show you our room! You'll be with me and Ruth and Edith and Ingrid."

The bedroom had two bunk beds and a small army cot wedged against the wall. Gina pulled open a large drawer and pushed some clothes to the side.

"Where is everyone?" Lisa asked.

"Working! You'll have to get a job, too, you know. I'm only here because I help Mrs. Cohen on Fridays as she prepares for Shabbat."

Gina showed her the bathroom—only one for all seventeen girls. She began listing rules: lights out at ten thirty, no food allowed in the bedrooms (for fear of mice), hot bath once a week (to save coal), chores on Saturday...

Lisa could hardly keep her eyes open. She offered a weak thank-you before falling onto the cot for a nap.

She awoke to the sound of thirty-two children, aged ten to seventeen. German and Yiddish and Czech and English mixed together in the hall. "I let you nap as long as I could!" Gina said. "We can't be late for Shabbat."

Shabbat! By now, Lisa had gone six months without it. Jumping up, Lisa combed her hair, smoothed her skirt the best she could, and ran downstairs.

♫

Mrs. Cohen lit the candles. As Lisa recited the Shabbat prayers along with the other children seated at two long tables in the dining room, she wanted to cry. It was the first time she had seen someone other than her mother light the candles, and she ached to be with her again.

Later, during dinner, Mrs. Cohen tapped her fork against her water glass. "We have a new girl tonight: Lisa Jura. She is from Vienna. Please take time after dinner to introduce yourselves to her."

Mrs. Cohen then asked if anyone had news to share.

"My parents have written to say they are no longer in Berlin," said a boy named Paul. "Their apartment has been taken away. They are looking for visas to Shanghai in China. I hope my brother will be coming soon on the train."

As they all listened, the children thought of their own parents, their own nightmare, their own hope.

After dinner, Gina took Lisa's arm and led her to the sofa to gossip.

"See the boys playing chess? The one facing us is Günter. He's got a crush on me, but I'm still deciding."

The front door opened and a handsome sixteen-year-old wearing a leather jacket walked in. Gina waved at him.

"Aaron, come here a minute; meet the new girl," said Gina. "This is Lisa."

That evening, Lisa received a parade of nice faces and polite words. Only one boy in the corner stayed away, writing in a notebook. He was more than six feet tall, with gigantic, muscular arms.

"That's Johnny, otherwise known as Johnny 'King Kong,'" Gina said, snickering.

"Johnny what?" Lisa asked.

"Didn't you see the movie *King Kong*? King Kong is a big ape just like him!"

"That's not very nice," Lisa said.

"It's just a nickname, silly."

But Lisa still resolved to be nice to the hulking boy with the serious face.

Soon it was ten thirty and lights-out. Lisa fell asleep with Gina still gossiping next to her.

♫

The next morning, Gina took Lisa to Platz & Sons, the garment factory where she worked. It was a three-story brick building and the air was stale and filled with dust. Scores of women bent over long rows of sewing machines. Gina hoped there would be a job for Lisa.

"Mr. Dimble, I know how to sew because my father is a tailor." When he asked Lisa to demonstrate, she sat confidently at the machine and produced a perfectly straight seam.

"You're hired," Mr. Dimble said. "Come back tomorrow morning, and we'll set you up."

Elated, Lisa took the London Underground train back to Willesden station and arrived in time for lunch. After the plates were cleared, she quietly walked to the piano and gently pulled back the shawl that covered it. She lifted the lid, sat down, and began the Grieg Piano Concerto in A Minor. The children arrived home soon after, and they silently gathered in the living room and on the stairs to listen.

Lisa was still playing when Mrs. Cohen came through the door, carrying a box of groceries. She stopped and stared at the young girl who was lost in her music.

"Listen to Lisa!" Edith said proudly to Mrs. Cohen.

Mrs. Cohen nodded and kept walking.

"Play something else, please?" asked Günter, coming over to stand by her side.

As Lisa launched into her favorite, "Clair de Lune," she watched Gina come in the door, followed closely by Aaron.

The room grew quiet, everyone focused on the beauty of the music.

♫

Mrs. Cohen asked to see her after dinner.

"I see you've studied the piano," she said, closing the door behind her.

"Yes, ma'am," Lisa answered.

"And would you like to practice while you're here?"

Unsure of how to answer, Lisa decided to speak from her heart. "I would very much like to, if you—"

Mrs. Cohen interrupted her to say that she had a son, in a special school, who would soon be coming to the hostel to live. "He also plays the piano. You may practice for an hour when you come home from work. If you like, you may play popular songs for us on Sunday."

"Thank you, ma'am."

Chapter Five

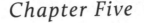

At Platz & Sons, Lisa was assigned to work on men's pants. She was given a sewing machine next to a quiet woman named Mrs. McRae and told to work fast. By the end of a day, her arms ached and her fingers were sore.

While she was grateful to be busy, thoughts of her sister Sonia were never far from her mind.

By this point, almost ten thousand children had come to England on the Kindertransport. Bloomsbury House assured Lisa again and again that Sonia was on the list. But there was still no word on a sponsor.

One day, Mr. Hardesty's secretary handed Lisa a letter that had just arrived from Vienna—the stamp on the front had a picture of Adolf Hitler. Lisa quickly ripped into the envelope.

> *Dear Liseleh,*
> *I am afraid I have no good news to*
> *report, except that we are in good*
> *health. I hope you are practicing your*
> *music. I will send remembrances*
> *from home so you do not forget us.*
> *Love, Mama*

Forget them! How could she forget them? They were her very soul.

At dinner, Lisa shared her worries about Sonia.

"Where is she?" Günter asked.

"Still in Vienna. She has a place on the train, but they haven't found a sponsor."

"You should do what Paul did," Günter said. "Paul! Come here!" The blond boy hurried over and squeezed in beside them.

Paul's brother was still in Munich, and to get help, Paul tried calling everyone in the phone book with the same last name as his.

"Why?" Lisa asked, not yet understanding.

"I told them I thought they were my relatives! Who knows, maybe they are."

Lisa's eyes lit up. She would try it!

"I'll help," Aaron offered.

"So will I," said Gina.

"Me too," Günter chimed in.

After rushing through dinner, the group leaned over the heavy phone books of London Northwest.

"We'll each call four of these numbers tomorrow," Gina offered.

"We'll call ourselves the Committee for the Resolution of All Ills," Aaron pronounced.

Aaron put his hand in the middle of the table, and Gina, Paul, Günter, and Lisa put their hands on top of his. "We're the committee, right?"

"The committee we are!"

Mrs. Cohen let Lisa switch her practicing to the hour after dinner so that she could knock on doors after work. But it didn't go as she hoped: No one said yes.

The people at work couldn't help—they were all as poor as she was. Still, she'd never give up—she'd get Sonia out no matter what.

♫

Lisa was walking back to the hostel one afternoon when a voice stopped her.

It was Mrs. Canfield, a Quaker woman who lived next door. She was dressed in black and leaning on a large wooden-handled rake.

"I have too many cucumbers and tomatoes this week," Mrs. Canfield said. "Would thou take them to Mrs. Cohen for me on thy way?"

"Of course," Lisa said politely, surprised at the Quaker woman's strange English.

While gathering cucumbers, Lisa gave in to temptation and bit into a juicy tomato. Mrs. Canfield walked out just as the warm juice exploded over Lisa's chin and blouse.

Quakers, members of a Christian movement known for their open-minded practices, were credited with helping many during World War II—including Jewish refugee children—with housing, education, and job training.

Frustrated, and now embarrassed, Lisa burst into tears.

"Don't worry," the woman said, before realizing that there was a deeper concern. "What's the matter?"

Lisa hesitated, then spoke. "My sister is still in Vienna. Please, do you know anyone that could help us be a sponsor?"

Mrs. Canfield promised to do all she could.

Two days later, Mr. Hardesty called to say that a Quaker family in the north of England had agreed to sponsor Sonia. When she learned that her sister would be on the train within the week, Lisa was delirious with joy.

♫

On Friday, September 1, 1939, Lisa came home early for Shabbat. The total blackout of London had been ordered. People began gathering supplies and hanging black curtains in the windows so that no light would shine through.

On the radio that evening, they heard that one million Nazi soldiers had marched across the border from Germany with lightning speed, headed for Warsaw, Poland. A new word was added to the vocabulary—*Blitzkrieg*, meaning "lightning war" or a method of quick and intense attack during war.

The following morning, the nuns from the convent next door brought over boxes of food. "We're leaving," they said. "But while we're gone, please use our basement." The air raid warden had told them it was a good bomb shelter.

Mrs. Cohen thanked the sisters. As they were leaving, one turned to Lisa. "Thank you for the beautiful music. We'll miss it."

"Thank you," Lisa said.

Later, Mrs. Cohen pulled Lisa aside. "I understand that Mrs. Canfield has friends who will take Sonia, but it may be difficult for them to take you, too," she said. "We would be willing to tighten our belts a little bit, if you'd like to stay."

Lisa bowed her head. "Thank you very much."

Then Mrs. Cohen handed her a stack of sheet music: Chopin and Schubert and Tchaikovsky! A name was penciled neatly on the top of each book: *Hans Cohen*.

"Thank you so much, ma'am!" Lisa cried.

♫

Lisa waited patiently at the train station. Her eyes searched for Sonia among the children that crowded the platform. When Lisa saw her frail and serious-looking thirteen-year-old sister come down the steep steps of the train, she ran to meet her and grabbed her tightly in her arms. "Sonia, Sonia, you've come, Sonia!"

As they held each other, it almost felt as if they were home in Vienna again.

At a café on the second floor, Lisa proudly showed off her English by ordering tea and sandwiches. Sonia presented her with a package: a silver evening purse that had belonged to their grandmother and a book of preludes by Chopin—the one her mother had helped her learn. It seemed like yesterday.

There was also a letter: *Lisa, take good care of our littlest treasure and know that all our prayers are for the day when we will be reunited.*

Attached to the letter was a photograph of their father, Abraham. Lisa was so grateful: It was getting harder to remember what he looked like.

Soon Mr. and Mrs. Bates from Norwich came to collect Sonia. They offered reassuring words about their farm and about their daughter, who was Sonia's age.

The sisters hugged goodbye. "The minute the bombing is over, you'll come to London with me, I promise," said Lisa.

"I promise!" she repeated as she watched the three of them disappear.

♫

The next morning, the residents of 243 Willesden Lane once again huddled around the radio to learn that Britain was declaring war on Germany. The rest of the day was spent preparing the bomb shelter in the basement next door. They dragged down food, supplies, mattresses, and blankets. They set up cozy corners where they would sleep.

Paul's face looked pale. He'd just learned that no more transports would be allowed to leave "Greater Germany." No more sisters and brothers would be coming until the end of the war.

Lisa had been the lucky one—Sonia had arrived on the very last train.

Chapter Six

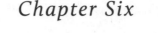

The British feared that the Nazis would be arriving at any moment. Platz & Sons switched to full-time production of uniforms, and as a result Lisa now cut and stitched pants for the Royal Navy—the British armed forces at sea. Rationing was announced on New Year's Day 1940. When Mrs. Cohen went to pick up their supplies, they were now mostly parsnips, potatoes, and flour. Often, Lisa felt hunger gnawing at her stomach.

One snowy Saturday, Lisa and Gina did the shopping. When they came home, they found a boy in his early teens on the couch. He had neatly combed hair and was wearing dark glasses.

"This is my son, Hans," said Mrs. Cohen. "He was hoping you could play something for him."

"Hello," Lisa said shyly.

"He will be staying at the hostel with us," Mrs. Cohen said, then turned and left them alone.

"Thank you for the use of your music. I hope you didn't mind," Lisa said.

"I won't be needing it," he said. "Would you play something by Debussy?"

"'Clair de Lune'?" she offered, launching into her favorite piece.

When it was over, Hans said, "Mother was right. You play beautifully."

"Won't you play me something now?" she asked.

There was a long silence before he spoke. "Yes, I will, if you'll help me to the piano."

It was only then that Lisa realized Hans was blind. She led him to the piano.

"Will you please show me middle C?" he asked.

She put his thumb on the proper key. Then,

hesitantly, he began to play with warmth and determination.

From then on, Hans joined Lisa at the piano bench each evening. He tapped his cane to the rhythm and offered praise and suggestions.

After each session, they listened to the radio. One night, almost all of the thirty residents crowded together to hear the words of the new prime minister of Britain, Winston Churchill. He announced that the Germans had broken through the French defenses. That night, Lisa went to bed trembling with fear. She pulled out the pictures of her mother and father and held them close as she fell asleep.

Winston Churchill became prime minister of Britain during World War II. Churchill gave many famous speeches that inspired courage and hope, even during the most difficult moments of the war.

Soon after, Lisa received two letters. One was news from Sonia, and the other was her own letter to her parents in Vienna, addressed to 13 Franzensbrücken Street. It had been sent back stamped UNDELIVERABLE. None of the "committee" members—Günter, Gina, Paul, Aaron, or Lisa—had received any recent news of their parents, either.

The five friends decided to ask at Bloomsbury House for answers about their families. Lisa handed Mr. Hardesty a handwritten list with their parents' names. "Please, can you find out where they are?"

After reading it, he leaned back in his chair. "We know very little. All we know is that many Jews are being sent to relocation camps, and that is why you are not receiving letters."

"Camps?" Gina asked.

"Relocation camps. We know very little about them. I'm sorry. Now, if there are questions about England, I'd be—"

WHAT WERE
CONCENTRATION CAMPS?

The Nazis were threatened by anyone who was different from them. The Nazis unfairly targeted people based on religion, ethnicity, sexual orientation, mental ability, and other factors. Shortly after taking power in Germany, the Nazis created concentration camps. In 1938, the Nazis began sending Jews to these prison camps, where they lost their freedom and many lost their lives. Prisoners in these camps received little food and were forced to perform slave labor.

Aaron rudely stood up and headed for the door. The rest followed, but Lisa stayed for a second.

"Thank you, Mr. Hardesty," she said.

♫

When Lisa and Gina went to work the next day, the newspaper headlines reported the worst: PARIS FALLS TO THE NAZIS. German forces had already taken over much of western Europe, so the fall of France left Britain to face Hitler alone. The British expected an invasion and prepared themselves.

One evening, Lisa noticed Johnny sitting on a milk crate near the back of the house, writing in his notebook by candlelight.

"Johnny! What are you doing?" Lisa asked.

"When I can't sleep, I write," he said nervously.

"May I see?" Lisa asked, leaning over to look, but Johnny put his huge hands over the page to cover it.

"It's not any good," he insisted.

"Maybe you'll show me some other time," Lisa said.

The children of Willesden Lane stayed up late into the night. Lisa grew bored watching Aaron and Hans endlessly playing chess, Hans beating him almost every time. "Have you always been blind?" she asked Hans.

He moved his pawn and sighed. "No, this happened last year."

"Last year?"

"A mob at school attacked me the day after Kristallnacht and blinded me. The doctor said it was a gift."

Confused and shocked, Lisa asked, "Why did he say that?"

"Because it got my mother and me out of Germany," he said. "Otherwise we might still be there."

The room was silent for a moment. Then Hans put his hands on the chessboard again and made his move.

"Checkmate."

♫

The following evening, Johnny slipped Lisa a piece of paper. Lisa opened the envelope and read: *Please do not show this to anyone else.* She unfolded a poem.

Always I see the faces
The faces at the station
The faces at the station
Are dimming before my eyes...

Always I hear the voices
The voices that are calling
That are calling out to me
But yet I cannot answer.

My mother, my father,
My sister, my brother
They are here now
Always
My heart is with them.

She looked up and saw Johnny staring at her from across the room. The poem moved her in the way that music usually did. She winked at him and folded the paper neatly in her pocket. He smiled back, raising his pen as a salute.

Chapter Seven

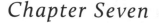

On September 7, 1940, the London Blitz began. Wave after wave of bombs struck the East End of London, right in the neighborhood of Platz & Sons. Over the next forty-eight hours, the children of Willesden Lane went back and forth into the shelter at all hours.

Lisa, Gina, and the other workers started leaving early so that they could be home before the alarms went off again. Lisa grabbed as many precious minutes on the piano as she could before another siren would blast.

Everyone wanted to help the war effort. Johnny announced that he had signed up for the "rescue squad"—even though he was fifteen and technically too young. Lisa wondered what she could do. She wasn't strong like Johnny, but she could play music. Suddenly it hit her: She could give people hope. She would organize a little concert, a "musicale," and invite refugees from another hostel. Mrs. Cohen gave her approval.

The musicale was scheduled for New Year's Day 1941, and all the children did their part to help and prepare. Gina planned to sing, while other friends borrowed musical instruments.

On December 29, in the middle of evening rehearsal, the air raid siren sounded once again. Everyone grabbed their things and headed underground—everyone but Lisa! She was playing with such determination that she couldn't hear that the bombs were coming closer.

Suddenly, the glass of the bay window shattered. Thrown by the force of the blast, Lisa lay on the floor, covered in dust and splinters, confused. But her fingers moved, and so did her arms! Instead of being terrified, she suddenly felt calm. *These bombs can't hurt me!* she told herself.

Aaron and Günter ran in. "Lisa! Are you all right?" they yelled together.

As another wave of airplanes approached, Aaron and Günter each took hold of one of her arms, lifted her up over the glass, and carried her back to the shelter.

A relieved Mrs. Cohen embraced Lisa in a huge hug. Then she turned to her and said,

"War is not the time to take foolish risks, young lady! You could have all been killed! Never, never do that again!"

Too overwhelmed to explain, Lisa apologized. When they emerged six hours later, smoke hung in the air with the dust and fog. Four houses on the block, including the hostel, had been hit. A hole ripped through their roof, and windows were completely blown out.

When the firemen said it was safe, Lisa and a dozen others rushed back into the building.

"Be careful, there's broken glass all around!" Mrs. Cohen yelled, but nothing she said could stop them.

Lisa ran to her bureau and pulled out her pictures, still intact, not even damp from the fire hoses. She read for the millionth time, *From the mother who will never forget you.*

"I'm safe, Mama," she whispered. Then she felt a gentle tug at her sleeve.

"Please hurry, Lisa, pack your things, we have to go," Mrs. Cohen said.

The thirty-two children were led to the community shelter to spend the night. They were officially homeless once again.

♫

"I have done my best to find you homes close to Willesden Lane until our home is livable again," Mrs. Cohen told the group.

"Unfortunately, some of you will be placed outside of London temporarily."

For the next hour, the housemates and friends left one by one. First Gina, then Günter, then Aaron.

"Lisa Jura," Mrs. Cohen said finally, and the Quaker lady dressed in black stepped into the foyer. Lisa looked up at her, surprised. This woman had done so much for her already!

"Will thou forgive me for being so late?" said Mrs. Canfield. She took Lisa's hand and helped her gather her belongings. Together they walked to Lisa's new home.

"I'm sure it is difficult being separated from thy friends, but I will try to make thee a home nonetheless," said Mrs. Canfield kindly.

♫

The months passed. One night, as Lisa lay in bed at Mrs. Canfield's, she heard a whistling at her bedroom window. She jumped up and saw Aaron outside.

"Meet me tomorrow for lunch: Trafalgar Square at noon."

Lisa protested. She usually had only fifteen minutes to eat. "Not unless you tell me why." Aaron paused for suspense, then told her: "Myra Hess."

Lisa jumped for joy at the thought of seeing Myra Hess, the famous English pianist, who was known for her unforgettable performances that raised the country's spirits during the war.

The next day she made up an excuse for leaving work, took the tube to Trafalgar Square, and met Aaron at the huge bronze lion statues nearby.

Together they ran across the street and into the imposing National Gallery, where a mammoth nine-foot grand piano sat at one end. They rushed to find seats among the hundreds of music lovers.

The bell-like tone of the Steinway grand filled Lisa's heart. For an instant, her childhood fantasy of a concert hall performance of her own seemed almost real.

As she watched for the next forty minutes, Lisa lived a thousand dreams. She hated when the beautiful notes slipped away. There was so much she wanted to say to Aaron, but she was needed back at the factory. She gave him a hurried thank-you hug and ran for the bus.

Chapter Eight

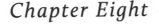

Crocuses came up in the front yard of 243 Willesden Lane in the spring of 1941, just in time for the reopening of the hostel.

"I promise I'll come visit," Lisa told Mrs. Canfield as they said goodbye out front.

"My house will always be thy house," Mrs. Canfield replied.

The hostel on Willesden Lane sparkled like new. But where was the piano? Had it been damaged?

"Surprise!" yelled a group of teenagers led by Johnny, Aaron, and Günter.

They pushed Lisa down the hall and into the kitchen. The door to the cellar was standing open, and through it Lisa spied the sturdy old upright piano.

"It's not the Royal Albert Hall," said Mrs. Cohen. "But if you insist on playing through the bombings, you should at least play where it's safe."

Afterward, Mrs. Cohen came over to Lisa. "Please come to my room before dinner, I want to talk with you about something."

Lisa prayed that it was not any bad news about the many things she always worried about—her parents, Rosie, and Sonia.

When it was time, she found Mrs. Cohen sitting on the bed with an open copy of the *Evening Standard* newspaper.

"I've been saving this to show you," Mrs. Cohen said, pointing to a small announcement in the middle of the page.

It read: "Auditions for admission and study at the Royal Academy of Music. Applications being accepted until April 1. Open to all students with a proficiency in musical performance of the classical repertoire."

The London Royal Academy? This was where the great musicians studied; this was where Myra Hess herself had studied!

"Would you like to apply for an audition?" Mrs. Cohen asked.

Would they let a refugee girl go to the Royal Academy? Lisa wondered. Then she remembered the phrase "make something of yourself." She knew this would make her mother so proud.

"Yes, ma'am," she answered firmly.

♫

During dinner, Lisa was given a letter with the words REPUBLICA DE MEXICO on the stamp. She didn't recognize the name on the return address.

Nervous, she asked Aaron to open it and read it for her.

Dear Lisa,
My name is Alex Bronson. I am
your brother-in-law Leo's cousin.
I am writing you to see if you have
any information regarding Leo and
Rosie, as we have lost contact with
them since their escape to Paris.

"Paris? They made it to Paris?" Lisa asked, relieved and worried at the same time. Aaron continued reading.

They traveled to Antwerp, Belgium,
where my father helped smuggle
them to France. Our visas came
through, and we left for Mexico.
That was eight months ago, and we
have had no news of them since.

Lisa let out a sob. "Go on," she said.

We pray Leo and Rosie have been
able to leave France because we
are receiving news that Jews are no
longer safe there.

Lisa shivered, hoping they had not been harmed.

Chapter Nine

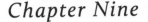

Lisa told her supervisors at Platz & Sons of her plans to apply for an audition. She asked if she could leave work a little early to practice.

"Three o'clock it is, then, but no slacking off before that, my girl!" said Mr. Dimble.

After work, she went to the Royal Academy of Music to pick up the application. There she studied the young men and women rushing by her. Their conversations included words such as *art* and *soul* and *beauty*. It was all too wonderful.

Back at Willesden Lane, she and Hans discussed the list of music pieces—a repertoire—that would best show off her skills.

With Hans's help, Lisa picked a few pieces by Bach and Beethoven. As they discussed the last selection, Hans remembered the stack of records in the room.

"Find me the Rubinstein recording. I want you to hear Chopin's Ballade in G Minor."

As she listened, Lisa felt nervous about the difficult chords. Still, hearing the power behind Rubinstein's performance, she nodded. "Yes, this is the piece."

♫

Lisa tried to avoid the news headlines and focus on sight-reading and fundamentals. *If only Professor Isseles could be here to help*, she thought. Yet it wasn't really the professor she missed. Some nights she would put her head on the keyboard and cry, "Mama, why can't you be here to help me?"

Hans helped Lisa practice sight-reading so that she could perform unfamiliar pieces on the spot. Since he had memorized every note of his own sheet music, he would instruct Aaron to choose a piece that Lisa hadn't seen before but which he knew perfectly. Aaron, who had studied the violin as a child, helped her with music theory—the rules behind the "language" of music.

The autumn and winter months were miserable for Lisa. She was working hard, and the cold was relentless. Plus, Aaron, who had become her companion, left the hostel after a heated argument with Mrs. Cohen about the curfew.

Lisa developed a cough so bad that sometimes Mrs. Cohen could hear it through the closed door of the cellar. One night, as Lisa practiced downstairs, there was a knock on the door. Mrs. Canfield stepped carefully down the stairs, followed by Johnny, who was carrying a small, old-fashioned coal-burning stove. Lisa recognized it from her time at Mrs. Canfield's house.

After protesting, Lisa thanked them, knowing the warmth would help.

The air raid siren soon sounded, and they all huddled together in the basement. Lisa shivered and started to cry. Mrs. Canfield put her arm around the girl.

"Sometimes I miss my family so much that I feel I can't go on," Lisa said, weeping. "I don't even know why I should go on without them."

Mrs. Canfield hugged the trembling girl tightly. "Ultimately, God is in charge of our world," she said. "I believe it is His will for thee to play thy music."

"My mother told me to always hold on to my music."

"You must go forward with that in thy heart, Lisa."

♫

Soon after, Lisa was diagnosed with bronchitis, a very bad cough. She awoke from a long, feverish dream to hear Mrs. Cohen say she must stay in bed and drink soup for a week.

"But I have to practice," Lisa said.

"Not until you're better, that's an order," said Mrs. Cohen.

Little did Lisa know that she'd already been asleep for two days! "You've missed everything," Gina said. Mrs. Cohen explained that the American naval base of Pearl Harbor had been bombed, and that the United States had joined the war.

Gina then began to cry. Johnny had been badly hurt and was in the hospital, she said.

He had been helping to put out a fire when a wall gave way.

"Oh no! Can I go see him?" Lisa asked.

"You are not to get out of bed," Mrs. Cohen said firmly.

Lisa turned away from them to control her emotions. *What a terrible thing this war is,* she thought as she prayed for her friend.

Chapter Ten

After two weeks of bed rest, Lisa was over her fever and back to a modified practice schedule. A week before the audition, Lisa went to see Johnny in the hospital.

"I have a request," Johnny asked. "When you play the Chopin, will you think of me?"

Lisa took his huge hands in her own. "Of course! I only wish I could play it for you right now."

"You don't have to. All I have to do is close my eyes and I can hear it."

Lisa kissed him gently on the forehead and left.

♪♪

With three days to go before the audition, Lisa arrived to work at Platz & Sons and found a package sitting on her chair.

"What's this?" she asked.

Several of the other ladies stood up and gathered around, saying nothing.

Mrs. McRae looked up from her work with a sneaky grin, as if she didn't understand the question.

Lisa carefully unwrapped the package and pulled out a beautiful dark blue dress. "Mrs. McRae, you didn't..." Stunned, Lisa held it up, and the ladies around her clapped.

♫

On the day of her audition, Lisa and Günter approached the grand entrance of the Royal Academy of Music. Seeing the large group of well-dressed English teenagers and their parents, Lisa felt her stomach drop.

The boys looked cool and confident. The girls wore simple, elegant black dresses. Lisa was proud of her own blue dress. Still, she stood apart: On this important day, she was the only aspiring musician who wasn't accompanied by her parents.

Don't worry, Mama, she said silently. *I know you're here.*

Lisa and twenty other students were taken to a small classroom on the third floor. They were handed pencils and test booklets and told they had one hour to complete the music theory portion of the exam.

Next, Lisa went to a practice room with an upright piano, to be tested on pitch.

Finally, her name was called for the performance section. She walked through the huge auditorium toward the stage, where a beautiful Steinway grand piano stood waiting.

She climbed the stairs, walked over to the piano, and bowed to the three judges.

Then she sat down, took a deep breath, and began her first selection, Beethoven's *Sonata Pathétique*.

The opening notes were serious and

heartfelt. Lisa imagined the care her mother took to kindle the flame of Shabbat. As her hands flew lightly up and down the keyboard, she imagined Sonia scurrying in and out with the plates for the Sabbath meal. Her hands searched for just the right touch to convey the sadness that lay within her.

"Thank you," she heard. The judges had let her go on for ten whole minutes!

She played two more selections until all that was left was the last piece Hans had suggested: Chopin's Ballade in G Minor.

Lisa's mother had told her that in this ballade, the composer, Chopin, was crying for the loss of his native Poland—having to flee the war and never to return. Lisa's fingers sang of her home of Vienna, Austria, now lost to her. She played for her parents, for Rosie, and even for Sonia, so far away.

Another thank-you pulled her back to

reality. The male judges were writing in their books, and the tiny woman nodded her head politely.

"That is all, you may go," they said. She bowed politely and walked off the stage.

Chapter Eleven

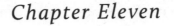

In the spring of 1942, eighteen-year-old Lisa started working overtime at the factory— partly out of patriotic duty and also to distract herself from waiting for the results of the audition.

The news across Europe was frightening and hard to believe. Some said there would be massive deportations of Jews from all over Europe. Most of the children at the hostel had stopped receiving letters from their parents in Europe. Instead, they focused on waiting for news on Lisa's audition.

"Lisa Jura?" Mrs. Cohen said one Friday night at the Shabbat meal, holding up a letter. "It's from the London Royal Academy of Music."

Lisa stared at it, paralyzed.

"Would you like me to open it?" Mrs. Cohen asked.

Lisa nodded.

Mrs. Cohen opened the letter, unfolded the thick, elegant stationery, and read: "'The Associated Board of the London Royal Academy of Music is pleased to inform Miss Lisa Jura that'"—from the end of the table came a scream from a young boy, who quickly had a hand slapped over his mouth—"'she has been accepted into the program for the study of the pianoforte.'"

Lisa was enveloped by kisses, hugs, and

thumbs-up signs. Those who couldn't get close enough clapped. She was a hero, and the children of Willesden Lane desperately needed a victory.

She put her arms around Mrs. Cohen. "I never would have known about the audition if it weren't for you. How can I ever thank you?"

"You have thanked me. You've brought honor to this house," Mrs. Cohen replied. "We all need to dream, and tonight, everyone is living their dream through you."

♫

Aaron showed up at 243 Willesden. "We're going to celebrate," he told her.

Lisa ran upstairs, putting on her new pleated skirt and a chic blue blouse, topped by a stylish felt hat, and met him in the foyer. He whistled his approval, and off they went.

They jumped on a double-decker bus and stopped at the Parliament building, or what was left of it after the recent bombings.

There, an old gentleman waved. "Hello, Mr. Lewin!" he said, shaking Aaron's hand. The man unlocked a door and led them to some narrow stairs.

They climbed to the top, where Lisa saw a

giant clock with its inner workings and huge bells.

"It's Big Ben!" Aaron exclaimed.

"I can't believe it!" Lisa cried delightedly.

They were high above London, and below them stretched out the City, the House of Commons, the great dome of St. Paul's, and crowded, winding streets. The Thames River flowed peacefully and disappeared into the distance. And in that moment, Lisa dared to have hope.

♫

By the time the crocuses appeared in the spring of 1943, Lisa was fully absorbed in her studies. Her Royal Academy instructor was a master teacher with a strong reputation— Mabel Floyd, the same small lady who had been on the jury at the audition.

That first year brought many other changes in Lisa's life. After a long struggle, her dear friend Johnny died—a tragic loss, shared by everyone who had known him. Meanwhile, Aaron enlisted in the armed forces as a paratrooper, or military parachutist.

By summer, the Bates family finally agreed that it was safe enough to allow Sonia to come and visit with her older sister in London.

Lisa met Sonia at the train station and took her to all her favorite spots. At Buckingham Palace they strained for a glimpse of the princess. When they walked past Big Ben, Lisa confided that she had visited the top of the bell tower.

At night, they wondered to each other whether they would see their parents and Rosie again.

"I'm sure it will be soon," Lisa tried to assure her sister.

A short letter from Leo's cousin in Mexico reported no news from Leo or Rosie. *Most all Jews from Vienna have now been deported to detention camps in Poland*, Lisa read.

Neither Bloomsbury House nor the Jewish Refugee Agency nor anyone else had any information. All letters came back stamped UNDELIVERABLE.

♫

By 1943, Platz & Sons was making military accessories. The work was harder than before, and Lisa's tired fingers began to feel the strain from the difficult, repetitive work.

During her weekly classes at the Royal Academy, Mabel Floyd noticed a difference in Lisa's piano playing. Rubbing the painful muscles of her right forearm, Lisa confessed that she was sewing on the assembly line during the day.

"My, my, we'll have to do something about

that," responded the teacher briskly. "Go home and get some rest. I'll see you next week. There will be no assignment."

At the end of the following week's lesson, Professor Floyd handed Lisa a handwritten letter. "The Howard Hotel is looking for a pianist to entertain the soldiers. I believe the pay is reasonable and the work will be much more suitable."

Lisa drew in her breath—a little gasp of delight. "Oh, thank you! Thank you, Professor Floyd."

♫

"We're sorry to lose you," said Mr. Dimble, when he heard the news, "but good luck in show business."

"I'll be reading the newspapers, searching for your name, Lisa," said Mrs. McRae. I'll be reading the arts section!"

They hugged, and with no further ceremony Lisa left the life of the factory behind.

♪♫

The Howard Hotel was a bustling nightspot in the West End of London. It had a large restaurant, a ballroom for dances, and "entertainment in the lounge" six nights a week.

The crowd wanted the favorite tunes of the day, and Lisa's training in sight-reading paid off. Soon the entire room would sing along as Lisa played spirited versions of the latest wartime tunes.

Chapter Twelve

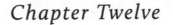

By 1944, the war was finally going the Allies' way. London was now crawling with soldiers—on the streets, in the theaters, and packed in at the Howard Hotel.

Tonight, Lisa was looking her best, excited to try out a piece by the composer Rachmaninoff—a selection she had learned in preparation for her upcoming year-end recital.

After the powerful ending, three soldiers led by a lieutenant approached Lisa, carrying a rose.

"Mademoiselle!" he said. "There is a gentleman who wants to meet you."

She followed them back to a table, where a tall man with compelling dark brown eyes stood up immediately. He held out his hand, and when she took it, he gracefully raised it to his lips and kissed it.

"*C'était magnifique! Que vous êtes magnifique!*"

"I'm sorry, I don't speak French," Lisa said.

"Rachmaninoff!" he said, cupping both hands over his heart.

"Ah, so you recognized the music!" She beamed at him. "You don't speak any English?" Lisa asked.

"His English is terrible," said his friend, speaking for him. "He's in the Resistance, fighting for the French forces. He's our captain."

The captain then said something in a deep voice to his lieutenant, who turned to Lisa and translated.

"He says to tell you that you are the most beautiful woman he has ever seen."

Intrigued, Lisa found herself believing it, just a little.

The captain looked into her eyes and said a few words in French.

The lieutenant translated: "He says you must promise to invite him if ever you give a concert. He says, no matter where he is, he will come."

The next night, the hotel was surprisingly empty. On her way home, Lisa looked up at the sky. Wave after wave of transport planes were flying away from the city. The Allied invasion of Europe had begun.

WHAT WAS THE ALLIED INVASION OF EUROPE?

This was a series of major military moves by the Allied forces that eventually led to the fall of Nazi Germany and the end of World War II in Europe. This includes D-Day, one of the largest military efforts in modern history.

While the Allies were fighting their way across Europe, they stumbled upon concentration camps. The Allies liberated the prisoners in these camps and helped the former inmates start their lives again.

♫

Professor Floyd clapped appreciatively at the end of Lisa's next rehearsal. "You are ready to soar!" she said, "It's time to think about your debut—your first grand performance."

Lisa was stunned; she said nothing.

"Usually, a student's family helps toward

the expenses of a debut, but because of your circumstances, the faculty has recommended that the academy help in the arrangements. That is, if you would like to make a debut," Professor Floyd said.

Lisa leaped from her seat, crying, "Of course I would!"

♫

As the battles in Europe raged ever more intensely, Lisa settled into a summer and fall of choosing and preparing a new repertoire for her debut.

She and her friends at Willesden Lane waited. Waited for letters, waited for word of their parents. Lisa tried to focus on her music. But one day, while practicing at the academy, she stopped at the sound of faraway bells—the chimes of Big Ben! The beautiful sound grew louder, joined by the bells of the churches throughout London.

The war was over!

Lisa joined a group of excited students running down the spiral staircase and into the streets. They boarded a packed trolley headed for Buckingham Palace. There, Winston Churchill himself was addressing the crowd.

"God bless you all. This is your victory!"

The king and queen and the princesses then appeared on the balcony, waving as the crowds cheered.

Staring at the joy on people's faces, Lisa was suddenly overcome with a shiver of isolation and sadness. When would the war be over for her? Or for her friends at the hostel?

♪♪

At first, there were just rumors—impossible rumors, which spread like wildfire through the already broken hearts of the Jewish community. Talk of murder, of unspeakable acts. Photos of dangerously thin people staring from behind barbed-wire fences, their bodies hardly able to stand, became public.

Lisa couldn't bear to hear what she was told. She had known the terror of the Nazis, had seen Kristallnacht, but never could she have imagined what had transpired, unreported, behind Nazi lines.

Every day, she went to the crowded hallways to study the lists of survivors that the Red Cross, the Jewish Refugee Agency, and the US Army taped to their walls.

There were no Juras on the lists. Lisa looked for Leo's name. There were dozens of Schwartzes, but no Leos and no Rosies.

WHAT WAS THE HOLOCAUST?

The Holocaust was the government-sponsored persecution and murder of six million Jews and millions of other victims. This unfair and cruel treatment was based on a person's identity, beliefs, or politics. The Holocaust lasted from 1933, when the Nazis took power in Germany, until 1945, when the Allied forces liberated Europe.

One weekend afternoon, a familiar figure walked through the front door of the hostel. It was Lisa's dear friend Aaron, carrying his Royal Air Force satchel and wearing the insignia of lieutenant.

Lisa asked him the difficult question: "Have you heard anything about your family, about your mother?"

He turned to her sadly. "Lisa, you must be realistic. What are the chances any of them survived?"

"Am I supposed to give up hope? Is that what you're saying?" Lisa asked, trying to sound brave. Could it be possible that she would never see her parents or Rosie again? How could she go on with her music without those whom she loved most in the world?

Aaron told her that he had managed to get a visa to America. He was trying to be positive—the journey to America gave him hope for the future.

But Lisa wasn't so sure. She could only stand sadly on the steps of the hostel, next to Günter and Gina, and wave goodbye as he left.

Chapter Thirteen

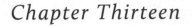

Months earlier, Günter had proposed to Gina while they were in the bomb shelter during one of the air raids. When their big day finally arrived, the handsome bride and groom celebrated at Willesden Lane.

Lisa put on her brightest face for the occasion. She was doubly happy, for Sonia had moved into the hostel the week before.

When the ceremony was nearly over,

Günter kissed his bride and stepped on a champagne glass to cries of "Mazel tov!" The assembly of well-wishers clapped, and Lisa performed a selection by the composer Grieg. When she was finished, Günter gave a toast to the friends and family lost to the war.

"May we remember the beauty of their gentle spirits and keep their memory in our hearts for the rest of our lives."

Feeling the sadness that had been cast by Günter's words, Mrs. Cohen hurried to bring out the cake. After the couple cut into it, Günter shared that he and Gina would be heading for New York as soon as his mother joined them. He was fortunate; his mother had survived the war. Gripped by the pain of another goodbye, Lisa hugged her friends.

♪♪

Children began arriving at the hostel from the "displaced persons" camps of Europe (temporary centers for refugees). Unlike the arrivals from Lisa's Kindertransport of 1939, these newcomers had gaunt eyes that had seen things not even an adult could bear.

Mrs. Cohen continued working at Willesden Lane, having found her calling. But Lisa was now twenty-one years old, and it was time for her and several of the others to make room for the younger children. Lisa moved in with Mrs. Canfield, the Quaker woman who had been kind enough to shelter her during the war.

♪

One week after Lisa's departure from Willesden Lane, Mr. Hardesty picked up Lisa and Sonia and took them to Liverpool station to meet the 2:22 train.

The doors opened, and a group of weary refugees appeared. Their faces were thin and tired, their coats ragged.

Finally, they heard a familiar voice shouting from down the quay.

"Lisa! Lisa! Sonia! Sonia!"

A thin, beautiful woman came running as fast as she could. It was Rosie, at last! The three sisters embraced and cried, calling out one another's names. When Lisa finally looked up, she saw Leo, patiently waiting his turn. She reached out, almost tripping on a four-year-old girl looking up at her in wonder.

Lisa gasped.

"This is our little Esther," Rosie announced. "Isn't she lovely?" Then, turning to the little girl, she said, "Esther, these are your aunties, Lisa and Sonia."

Lisa's eyes were so filled with tears she could barely see. Sonia knelt down and gave the little girl a kiss.

At the same café where Lisa had taken Sonia so long ago, Leo told the sisters how he and Rosie had survived the last few years. They escaped Vienna, traveled to Paris, and when Paris fell to Hitler, kept running and hiding.

The baby was born on the streets of France, Rosie explained. "Then we kept going until we made it to the Swiss border. We never gave up hope that we would see you again," Rosie whispered.

When Lisa shared that she was studying at the music academy, Rosie took Esther's hand

and told her daughter, "Your aunt Lisa is a wonderful pianist—just like your grandmother."

Finally, Lisa had to ask. "Rosie, do you have any news of Mama and Papa?"

Rosie looked at her sister with tears in her eyes.

"None of our letters were answered.... I have heard nothing," she answered. Then, sadly pleading, she asked, "So, then, you have heard nothing either?"

"Nothing," Lisa said. "We have heard nothing."

They could not bear to discuss it further. Rosie looked at her two younger sisters. "Mama would be so proud of you two," she said softly. "And, Lisa, you know what your music meant to her—to all of us? Look!"

Rosie leaned over and parted the buttons of Esther's coat. Around the little girl's neck was the chain that held the tiny gold piano charm.

"You have it?" Lisa cried, surprised.

Sonia spoke up. "I gave it to Rosie when I left on the train, just like you gave it to me."

Rosie put her arm around Sonia and said to Lisa, "And I never took it off, until I gave it to Esther."

The promise Lisa had made to her mother long ago now echoed in her heart. Over the next weeks, she returned to her piano, throwing all her energy and passion into her preparation. For how would the next generation know of the music, the music Malka so loved, if Lisa didn't honor her promise?

Chapter Fourteen

In the dressing room at Wigmore Hall, twenty-one-year-old Lisa tried to sit still as her sister applied a brown stripe above her eyelashes.

"Ooh, perfect!" said Rosie, putting on the last dab.

Sonia ran into the dressing room from the stage, where she had been peeking out at the crowd through a slit in the curtains.

"It's almost full!" she cried excitedly.

Of course, the students and faculty of the Royal Academy would be there. Rosie had invited every person she met—people on the street, the butcher on the corner. She also insisted that Lisa invite the handsome French soldier she met at the Howard Hotel. Lisa knew he would never come, but it didn't hurt to dream.

So much had changed since she had dreamed as a child of playing concerts in the royal halls of Vienna. After one more hug from her sisters, she was left alone. All was quiet, and the curtain began to rise.

Lisa walked onto the stage, greeted by enthusiastic applause. She took her seat at the nine-foot grand piano, and a hush fell over the room. Feeling the audience disappear, she lifted her hands in a graceful arch.

She started with Beethoven's *Sonata Pathétique*—softly, as her mother had often

counseled. The notes recalled the quiet sadness of being separated from her family.

Her many friends sat in the audience: Mrs. Cohen, Mrs. Canfield, Mrs. McRae, Mr. Dimble, Professor Floyd, Mr. Hardesty, Günter, Gina, and Hans. Lisa wove their stories through each piece she played, and the music became the tale of so many in war-torn London.

Lisa played her final selection, a piece by the composer Chopin. Through their tears, members of the audience remembered their proudest, bravest moments. They remembered their courage during the bombings. They remembered their determination. They remembered their ultimate victory.

After several seconds of awed silence, the audience erupted in applause. Lisa rose and the applause grew louder.

♪♩

In the dressing room, there was chaos: All the hostel children wanted to shake Lisa's hand, as did ten women from the factory, Mr. Hardesty and the staff of the Jewish Refugee Agency, and so many others.

Hans sat on a chair near Lisa. Next to him stood Gina and Günter. When the younger children of the hostel finished their congratulations, Mrs. Cohen pulled out her handkerchief and looked at them all.

"When did this happen? You are no longer children!" she cried.

Lisa, Gina, and Günter took her by the hand. "But we are," said Lisa. "We will always be the children of Willesden Lane."

At the stage door stood a handsome French Resistance soldier, waiting for the crowd to thin. He was carrying a dozen red roses.

He put his hands over his heart, then

handed her the red roses with a card that read: "With fervent admiration, Michel Golabek."

Lisa took his hand and brought him into the group of well-wishers. As happy as she was, she suddenly sensed an additional presence—as if her mother, Malka, were watching from above. Her heart filled with joy as she realized she had fulfilled the promise she made to her mother: She had held on to her music.

Epilogue

Aaron went to the United States, married, and became a successful businessman. Günter and Gina also immigrated to the United States, where they lived happily together for more than fifty years. Hans remained in England, received his degree as a physical therapist, and went on to win numerous national chess championships for the blind. After closing the hostel at Willesden

Lane, Mrs. Cohen lived with her son until her death at age seventy.

In the fall of 1949, Lisa Jura received a visa allowing her to immigrate to America. Michel Golabek, who had become one of the most decorated Jewish officers in the French Resistance, followed soon after. They were married in New York in November 1949. They moved to Los Angeles, joining Rosie and Leo, who had settled there, and were followed by Sonia and her husband, Sol. The sisters remained in daily contact for the rest of their lives.

In 1958, Lisa Jura was contacted by a long-lost cousin living in Israel, who wrote her with the truth of what had happened to her parents, Malka and Abraham. The cousin had received Abraham's last known communication, a letter that had been written in January 1941 and had been rerouted around the world to Palestine. Abraham wrote of their pending deportation and implored the cousin with the words *We are lost...and beg you to look after our precious children.*

On April 14, 1941, they were arrested by the Gestapo, taken from their home on Franzensbrücken Street, and deported to the city of Lodz in Poland. From there, they were sent to the Auschwitz concentration camp, where they were killed.

Lisa Jura had two daughters, Mona and Renée, who grew up to fulfill their mother's dream by becoming concert pianists. Lisa's three granddaughters, Michele, Sarah, and Rachel, also play the piano. Her grandson, Jonathan, plays the violin.

In June 1999, Lisa's daughters and granddaughters were invited to be the featured artists at the sixtieth worldwide reunion of the Kindertransport in London. Performing the "Clair de Lune" on the BBC, Michele and Sarah thanked Britain for saving Lisa's life and spoke of the precious words given to them by their grandmother and piano teacher: "Hold on to your music. It will be your best friend."

It continues to be.

Photographs

Lisa and her sister Sonia.

A Jura family photograph: baby Lisa, her father, Abraham; her mother, Malka; and her older sister, Rosie.

Mrs. Cohen and the children of Willesden Lane.

Lisa playing piano.

Lisa and her husband, Michel.

Acknowledgments

Heartfelt thanks to Jackie Maduff and Larry Kirshbaum, without whom this book would never have happened.

Thank you to Christine Burrill and Lee Cohen. Special thanks to Sarah J. Robbins for the beautiful abridgment of the original book.

Deepest appreciation to my wonderful editor, Alexandra Hightower, and the Little, Brown family for their amazing belief in and support of this story.

Thank you, Olga and Aleksey Ivanov for your wonderful illustrations.

Finally, my infinite love to Lisa's grandchildren—Michele, Sarah, Jonathan, and Rachel—who inspire me every day to go out into the world and share the precious message of their great-grandmother.

Discussion Questions
and Activities

1. An immigrant is a person who settles in a foreign country. A refugee is someone who flees his or her homeland and cannot return safely home. Was Lisa an immigrant or a refugee? What is the main difference between the meanings of the two words?

2. What challenges do refugees face in the world today? Think about your own experiences, and think about people you know or have read about.

3. Music plays an important role throughout Lisa's life. How does music help her during difficult times? What helps you during difficult times?

4. Lisa cherished the photograph of her mother that she brought to England. If you had to leave your home and were allowed to take only a few items of importance with you, what do you think you would take? What is the significance of the item or items you chose? Write a paragraph describing each item and what it means to you.

5. How did Lisa inspire the other residents of Willesden Lane? What other examples of inspiration have you encountered in this story? Who or what inspires you?

Historical Timeline
of the Holocaust

1933

After a democratic election, the National Socialist German Workers' Party, or Nazis, become the ruling party in Germany. Adolf Hitler is made chancellor, or prime minister, of Germany.

1935

The Nuremberg Laws, which deprive Jews of citizenship and other fundamental rights, are made legal.

1938

Nazi Germany takes over the Austrian Republic in an event known as the Anschluss.

Kristallnacht (the Night of Broken Glass) occurs on November 9–10. Nazis attack Jews in Germany, Austria, and the former Czechoslovakia.

Kindertransports begin taking Jewish and non-Jewish children to the safety of other countries.

1939

Germany occupies the remaining parts of the former Czechoslovakia and invades Poland.

World War II begins.

1940

In Nazi-occupied Poland, Nazis separate Jews from non-Jews by forcing them to live in designated parts of cities, known as ghettos.

Germany conquers the Netherlands, Denmark, Norway, Belgium, Luxembourg, and France.

The last Kindertransport arrives in Great
Britain by boat.

The German air force begins the massive
bombing of Britain known as the Blitz.

1941

Germany attacks their own ally, the Soviet
Union.

After the Japanese—a German ally—bomb
Pearl Harbor, the United States declares
war on Japan. Days later, Germany
declares war on the United States.

1942

Allied radio broadcasts report that the Germans are systematically killing the Jews
of Europe.

1945

The Germans surrender.

By the time the Holocaust is over, at least six
million Jews are dead.

A Deeper Look:
Understanding the Holocaust

The Spread of Nazism

In March 1938, Nazi Germany took over the Austrian Republic in an event that became known as the Anschluss, or "annexation." Once in power, the Nazis quickly passed German anti-Jewish laws, including the Nuremberg Laws, to exclude Jews from economic, cultural, and social life. By the summer of 1939, hundreds of Jewish-owned factories and thousands of businesses had been closed by the government.

Later in 1938, the horrifying acts of Kristallnacht took place. Afterward, the

German press described the violence as a "spontaneous reaction" of the German people, but this was not true. In fact, the government had carefully planned the attacks, with a list of buildings that would be allowed to burn. On top of the violence, the government unjustly fined the Jewish community one billion marks for "property damaged in the rioting."

The Effect of the Kindertransport

Many people around the world were outraged by the events of Kristallnacht, but only a few were willing to offer Jewish refugees shelter. Among them were a number of Jews and Christians in Britain and Nazi-occupied Europe. Organizations such as Bloomsbury House connected incoming refugees with private organizations that paid for each child's care, education, and eventual return home.

Unfortunately, once World War II began, the British banned all further immigration from Nazi-occupied countries.

The first Kindertransport train arrived in England on December 2, 1938. The last transport left on September 1, 1939, just hours before World War II began. In all, the operation saved nearly 10,000 children, about 7,500 of whom were Jewish. More than 1.5 million Jewish children were murdered during the Holocaust. The vast majority of children on the transports would be the only surviving members of their families.

Understanding this difficult history and reading about experiences such as Lisa Jura's can help us become active citizens in our communities today. Hopeful stories of survival, such as *The Children of Willesden Lane*, remind us of the importance of remembering the past and that we all have a role in building a better, brighter future.

Resources

Lisa of Willesden Lane and the middle-grade novel *The Children of Willesden Lane* have inspired a collection of rich educational materials now being used by teachers worldwide to expand students' knowledge of Holocaust history and their understanding of cultural differences, human perseverance, and the value of diversity through the music and story of Lisa Jura.

HOLD ON TO YOUR MUSIC FOUNDATION
Anchored in the inspiring story of Holocaust survivor Lisa Jura, the Hold On To Your Music Foundation fosters hope through the power of storytelling and music, enlightening people of all ages with the knowledge that we can flourish and our dreams can thrive, even when faced with immense adversity. Hold On To Your Music was established

in 2003 by Mona Golabek to share the story of her mother, Lisa Jura, as told in Ms. Golabek and Lee Cohen's book, *The Children of Willesden Lane*, and to disseminate the book and accompanying educational materials to students and teachers everywhere. Find out more about the Kindertransport and World War II with an expanded study guide, free musical selections, and classroom videos. Learn how to bring Mona Golabek to your community for a citywide Willesden Read.

holdontoyourmusic.org

USC SHOAH FOUNDATION

USC Shoah Foundation–the Institute for Visual History and Education develops empathy, understanding, and respect through testimony, using its Visual History Archive of more than 55,000 video testimonies, the award-winning IWitness education program, and the Center for Advanced Genocide Research. USC Shoah Foundation's interactive programming, research, and materials are accessed in museums and universities, cited by government leaders and NGOs, and taught in classrooms around the world. Now in

its third decade, USC Shoah Foundation reaches millions of people on six continents from its home at the Dornsife College of Letters, Arts and Sciences at the University of Southern California.
sfi.usc.edu

Find additional testimony-based resources, lessons, activities, digital tools, and other resources for multiple grade levels, languages, subject areas, and topics.
IWitness.USC.edu/willesdenlane

LOS ANGELES MUSEUM OF THE HOLOCAUST

Los Angeles Museum of the Holocaust, the first survivor-founded Holocaust museum in the United States, is a primary source institution that commemorates those who perished, honors those who survived, and houses the precious artifacts that miraculously weathered the Holocaust. The museum proudly houses the original artifacts and documents of Lisa Jura's story and her family.

lamoth.org

KORET FOUNDATION

The Koret Foundation is committed to strengthening the Bay Area and supporting the Jewish community in the United States and Israel through strategic grant making to outstanding organizations. Grounded in historical Jewish principles and traditions, and dedicated to humanitarian values, the foundation is committed to innovation, testing new ideas, and serving as a catalyst by bringing together people and organizations to help solve societal and systemic problems of common concern. The Koret Foundation is supporting a new global Holocaust educational program in partnership with USC Shoah Foundation and Hold On To Your Music Foundation. This new program will combine testimony, technology, and music, and alter the field of Holocaust education for primary- and secondary-school-aged children around the world.

koret.org

About the Authors and Illustrators

Mona Golabek is a Grammy-nominated recording artist, internationally celebrated concert pianist, star of the one-woman show *The Pianist of Willesden Lane*, and author of *The Children of Willesden Lane*, *Hold On to Your Music*, and *Lisa of Willesden Lane*. She has traveled the globe sharing her mother's inspirational message. Mona invites you to visit her online at holdontoyourmusic.org.

Lee Cohen is a journalist, screenwriter, and poet.

Olga and Aleksey Ivanov are renowned children's book illustrators and classically trained commercial artists from Russia who now reside in Denver, Colorado.